THE COGNITIVE BEHAVIOURAL CC POCKETBOOK

By Dorothy Spry

Drawings by Phil Hailstone

"A concise, informative and robust appraisal of CBC that captures the essential elements of theory, practice and research to present a most valuable contribution as to how CBC can be effectively applied. By incorporating emotional intelligence into the methodology of coaching techniques, Dorothy highlights its importance in the overall CBC coaching framework, adding a very practical and original dimension."

Dr Barry Cripps, C. Psychol

Published by:
Management Pocketbooks Ltd
Laurel House, Station Approach, Alresford, Hants SO24 9JH, U.K.
Tel: +44 (0)1962 735573   Fax: +44 (0)1962 733637
E-mail: sales@pocketbook.co.uk
Website: www.pocketbook.co.uk

The author wishes to thank Margaret Chapman, the author of the Emotional Intelligence Pocketbook, for her invaluable work and support.

This edition published 2010.   ISBN 978 1 906610 17 3

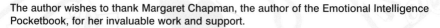

British Library Cataloguing-in-Publication Data – A catalogue record for this book is available from the British Library.

Design, typesetting and graphics by **efex ltd**. Printed in U.K.

CONTENTS

1NTRODUCTION

COGNITIVE BEHAVIOURAL COACHING APPROACH

This pocketbook is about a powerful and deceptively simple coaching approach, one that merges elements of psychology (cognitive behavioural therapy) with regular coaching practice. It is written both for coaches interested in incorporating a cognitive behavioural approach to their existing coaching toolkit and for managers and HR professionals who want to understand more about the way people's thoughts affect their decisions and actions.

CBC involves thinking about thinking, about the impact your thoughts can have on your life. To quote Epictetus, the Greek Stoic philosopher:

'We are disturbed not by events, but by the beliefs which we hold about them.'

The essence of this statement, that it is not events themselves that cause distress but the way that we interpret them and perceive them, is at the heart of cognitive behavioural approaches in coaching (CBC).

DEFINITIONS

Before we go any further, we need to define some terms:

- **Cognitive** refers to the mental processes that take place when we are thinking, everything that goes on in the mind including daydreams, past memories, present thoughts, immediate perceptions and thoughts about the future

- **Behaviour** refers to everything we do, every action and practical step that we take including talking, writing, driving, holding meetings, playing, making love, making music, all our actions and, paradoxically, our inactions

- **Coaching** is the process of helping, advising, encouraging, empowering and supporting other people (clients) to enhance their performance, and be more effective both at work and at home

AIMS OF THIS BOOK

This pocketbook gives sound and practical guidance based on the psychological theory surrounding cognitive behavioural therapy. It will help you facilitate change in yourself or your coaching clients in a systematic way that is both evidence-based and goal-focused. It will:

- Explain how emotions, feelings, thoughts and beliefs can cloud your judgement
- Explain how emotions, feelings, thoughts and beliefs can be used as the foundation stones for change
- Introduce you to CBC techniques
- Guide you through the ABCDE model
- Provide you with examples of real evidence-based coaching case studies
- Stimulate the importance of reflection in your own coaching practice

Note: The terms **coach** and **client** are used throughout the book as if the reader is a coach and actively engaged in the coaching process. The book can also serve, however, as a useful tool for reflecting on your own continuous professional development (CPD), whether or not you are a coach.

BENEFITS OF CBC

By using a CBC approach, the coach can help a client to identify, examine and change unhealthy thoughts, feelings and beliefs, and start them thinking in ways that are more realistic, positive and workably effective.

As well as helping develop healthy and productive behaviours, CB coaching contributes to the individual's overall emotional development.

- CB coaching can help clients reframe the way they think, feel and behave to bring about positive changes at work and in their personal life

- It works by changing the negative way that we think and feel about ourselves and the challenges we face, and turning these negative feelings around to positive thoughts, feelings and actions

- CB coaching is solution-focused – based on resolving *here and now* issues and offering an action plan

CBC IN DETAIL

CB coaching:

- Helps you support your client to control their emotions, thoughts and self-defeating beliefs

- Uses techniques that are supported by evidence-based psychological research

- Uses reason and reality testing to modify distorted and self-defeating ways of thinking

- Promotes a more flexible way of looking at personal and business related challenges

- Equips clients to tackle present problems as well as future challenges

- Can bring about enhanced feelings of well-being, as positive feedback is received from peers and management, thus reinforcing new behaviours

- Provides strategies to enable a client to become both emotionally aware and emotionally intelligent. By changing thoughts the client learns how to manage their emotions and feelings

- Has the goal of enabling the client to become their own coach

WHAT CBC IS NOT

✗ **Not just about positive thinking**

CBC is about more than this; it is about the client having positive thoughts, feelings, behaviours and **healthy attitudes** which enable them to **see life through a more balanced and realistic lens**, to solve problems and set themselves very well-defined goals.

✗ **Not just about unstructured goal setting**

CBC is about more than this; it is about setting goals in a very structured SMART way: **S** (specific), **M** (measurable, observable by others), **A** (attainable), **R** (realistic) and **T** (time-based).

✗ **Not about therapy, ie it's not a psychoanalytic approach that delves into repressed, past childhood memories**

Instead it adopts a client-centred coaching approach, focusing very much on the *here*, *now* and *future*.

We look next at how CBC differs from other coaching approaches.

HOW CBC DIFFERS FROM OTHER COACHING

There are many popular, highly practical coaching models around today. One good example is the **GROW** model, popularised by Sir John Whitmore. **G**oals, **R**eality, **O**ptions and **W**ill equip a coach to frame the coaching conversation by following an action plan, setting goals, and empowering the client to move towards goal attainment.

While the practical approach may be sufficient for clients wishing to focus on this aspect, it will not be enough if a client is experiencing a psychological or emotional barrier which is causing unhelpful goal blocking, or performance interfering emotions, thoughts, feelings and actions.

INTRODUCTION

HOW CBC DIFFERS FROM OTHER COACHING

CBC adopts a two-pronged approach, both **psychological** and **practical**, by tackling the self-defeating emotions, thoughts, feelings, philosophies and beliefs as well as using tried and tested practical and reflective techniques to help change behaviour.

In a nutshell, both these components of CBC make psychological ideas and techniques easily accessible to an experienced coach. They also help in building the bridge for the way the coaching industry is evolving – towards becoming a more psychologically evidence-based and scientist-practitioner approach.

ORIGINS OF CBC

There are several theoretical models for understanding and tackling psychological blocks that inhibit performance at work. Two of these influences are taken from the work of Albert Ellis (rational emotive behavioural therapy, REBT) and Aaron Beck (cognitive behavioural therapy, CBT).

Since the early 1960s, when both these approaches came into prominence, an abundance of evidence has accumulated demonstrating how effective they are in the treatment of: anger management, assertiveness, anxiety, stress and depression, with cognitive behavioural therapy (CBT) being the preferred choice, in the UK, of the National Institute for Clinical Excellence (NICE) and the National Health Service (NHS 2009 launch).

ORIGINS OF CBC

Cognitive behavioural coaching focuses on the idea that how we react to events is largely determined by the **beliefs** we hold about them, not by the events themselves.

Through examining and re-evaluating some of our less helpful **thoughts** and **beliefs** we can develop and try out new and alternative viewpoints and behaviours that may be more effective. As we receive feedback from friends, peers and managers, it reinforces, if positive, our new behaviours until they are hardened into our 'new self'.

The work of leaders in the CBC field – Windy Dryden, Stephen Palmer, Gladeana McMahon and Michael Neenan – has allowed for the smooth transition of psychologically based approaches from the therapeutic community into the organisational landscape.

This pocketbook also considers the additional dimension of *emotional intelligence* and its importance in CB coaching.

APPLICATIONS OF CBC

In the workplace, CBC may be used to resolve, for example:

- Anger management issues – unhealthy temper tantrums
- Anxiety over forthcoming events – such as giving a presentation
- Impatience –*'hurry up, hurry up! I wanted that job yesterday!'*
- Self-confidence – does a job well, but won't allow this to be true
- Indecisiveness – *'umm…what plan of action should I take?'*
- Procrastination – work avoidance behaviours
- Assertiveness – under or over assertiveness and its implications in the workplace
- Communication problems – interpersonal relationships and troublesome emotions resulting from poor emotional intelligence

In the next chapter we examine where the coaching profession stands today regarding the skill sets and standards of a good coach, and the reason why cognitive behavioural coaching is becoming increasingly influential as an approach.

BUILDING YOUR COACHING ARCHITECTURE

BUILDING YOUR COACHING ARCHITECTURE

SECOND TO THIRD GENERATION COACHING

The coaching industry has now mushroomed into a multi-million pound affair and is in the process of moving from a second to a more mature third generation profession.

With so many coaches now competing for business, and buyers of coaching becoming ever more conscious of the need to achieve return on investment, the bar for what makes a good coach has been raised.

There is also much debate from various quarters for higher standards in coaching, in what is currently an unregulated profession.

SECOND TO THIRD GENERATION COACHING

Appropriately accredited coaches will be familiar with the following seven principles that underpin their work to guide their clients through the process of change.

1. Set up a coaching contract which can be revisited.

2. Ensure appropriate boundaries of confidentiality are in place.

3. Express empathy through the use of reflective listening and summarising so the client feels they have been heard.

4. Use clean language questioning techniques (www.cleanlanguage.co.uk).

5. Develop discrepancy between the client's goals and current behaviour.

6. Roll with resistance rather than trying to confront a client who is not taking responsibility for their own behaviour change.

7. Support and encourage self-belief and optimism to change.

BUILDING YOUR COACHING ARCHITECTURE

SECOND TO THIRD GENERATION COACHING

GUIDELINES

To encourage increased professionalism and maturity of the coaching profession as a whole, we should also be considering the following guidelines:

- Evaluation of one to one coaching interventions using scientifically validated **psychometric tests** (pre and post) to establish what, if any, level of behaviour change took place

- Measurement of group coaching programmes using psychometric testing as the baseline measurement (pre and post), following this up with appropriate **evaluation**, ie statistical analysis after the coaching intervention to see what level of behaviour change, if any, took place

- Adoption of effective and proven **psychological theories** and **models** of coaching in which to broaden a coach's scope when working with different clients and their varying circumstances. This will enable a coach to alternate between current goal-based models such as **GROW** and CBC depending on the needs and circumstances of the client

SECOND TO THIRD GENERATION COACHING

GUIDELINES

- Create a showcase of **research studies**; there is remarkably little available at the moment. For example, Anthony Grant the director of the first coaching psychology unit (Australia), while conducting an in-depth review of literature published between 1938 and 2001, found that only 17 empirical evaluations of coaching interventions in non-clinical populations had been conducted

- Grant's review has inspired the call for more evidence-based practice in coaching to establish which coaching methods and interventions actually **work** and which **do not**

BUILDING YOUR COACHING ARCHITECTURE

YOUR COACHING VALUES

The following exercise allows coaches to reflect on what they currently offer in their toolkit and approach.

Consider the questions – they will help to point out those areas where you yourself might like to develop further.

1. What is your philosophy of coaching?

2. What values inform your coaching?

3. What ethical standards underpin or inform your practice?

4. What professional body do you subscribe to?

5. Are you in supervision?

BUILDING YOUR COACHING ARCHITECTURE

YOUR COACHING PRACTICE

1. What is your coaching process and approach?

2. What tools, eg psychometric tests, do you use?

3. What else do you do?

4. Does your coaching involve evaluation of effectiveness?

5. Does your framework integrate your own philosophy, underpinning theories, ethics, values, and beliefs?

YOUR COACHING PRACTICE

This pocketbook encourages coaches to take a step further in order to be part of a recognised and mature coaching profession, in which coaches adopt different psychologically proven models, theories and techniques.

As well as introducing you to the **ABCDE** model, the centrepiece of the cognitive behavioural coaching approach, the book also includes a **coach's toolbox** that demonstrates effective interventions when gauging a client's readiness for change, and gives guidance on setting realistic and **SMART** goals using the House of Change model.

In the chapter **evaluation of effectiveness**, we present three research studies that demonstrate the effectiveness of using psychologically proven CBC methods and interventions. A case study featuring an IT team leader is also used throughout the book to demonstrate the CBC approach.

We move now to considering the importance of self-awareness.

SELF-AWARENESS

SELF-AWARENESS

WHERE TO START

As the saying goes, '*you can lead a horse to water but you can't make it drink*'. Building the client's emotional self-awareness is an essential starting point.

Without your client knowing who they are, how they think, feel and behave, and how they come across to others in the workplace, they will find it extremely difficult to break through the barrier to their own growth and development.

A coach will often have to challenge ingrained personality traits, learnt behaviours and habits which have embedded themselves over a lifetime into the client's psyche. It comes as no surprise, therefore, that at times a coach may find it difficult to explore what will make their client actually see that a change is important. This is never a straightforward task; effective coaching is, however, measured by having the client recognise their current behaviour, and take action to change it into the new, agreed behaviours and to measurably improve their performance in the workplace.

We look next at how emotions and thoughts can interfere with the coaching process.

EMOTIONS & THOUGHTS

There is mounting evidence that **emotions** and **thoughts** are interdependent, and that this reciprocal relationship guides us to use appropriate learned behaviours in the pursuit of our goals. The wiring of the brain enables our emotions and thoughts to work together in unison.

Some coaches, when beginning their practice, may lack confidence in negotiating emotions within a goal and solution focused framework and therefore may treat emotions as peripheral. **Warning** – ignoring emotions can result in oversimplification of the issues and context, and be a hindrance to facilitating change in your client.

> *Emotions matter for rationality. In the dance of feeling and thought the emotional faculty guides our moment to moment decisions, working hand in hand with the rational mind, enabling or disabling thought itself. Likewise, the thinking brain plays an executive role in our emotions – except in those moments when emotions surge out of control and the emotional brain runs rampant.*
>
> **Daniel Goleman**, *Emotional Intelligence – Why it can matter more than IQ*, (1995).

ROLE OF EMOTIONAL INTELLIGENCE

We now look at the role that emotional intelligence plays in cognitive behavioural coaching. Emotional self-awareness is the chief building block of emotional intelligence. If the client cannot see what needs to be changed about themselves, how can they successfully manage other people's emotions?

The concept of emotional intelligence made its way from the psychology department into organisations back in the 1990s and still remains prominent today. To define emotional intelligence: it is the capacity for recognising our own feelings and those of others, for motivating ourselves, and for managing emotions well, in ourselves and in our relationships. If the client's feelings and thoughts, the emotional undercurrents, are not tackled, this acts only to stifle or block the client from moving forwards to reach their goals. Examples of emotional blockers are: *anxiety, anger, shame, hurt, guilt, depression, jealousy and envy*.

The example on the following pages shows how two individuals use their emotional intelligence and react to the same situation in very different ways.

RUDE OR PREOCCUPIED?

A manager came into the office this morning and walked right past her secretary without saying hello. This was interpreted by the secretary as rudeness, prompting negative and unhelpful automatic thoughts: '*I shouldn't be treated like that; what have I done to deserve it? I feel angry, upset and hurt*'.

Another individual, experiencing the same frosty and silent encounter, automatically thought, 'she must be busy, or preoccupied by something. I will have a chat with her later to see if everything is OK'.

The secretary caused herself an emotional disturbance by thinking she was being brushed aside by her manager without even a courteous 'hello'. As well as being upset, she was anxious about what had happened. This created further emotional turmoil, in that she was angry and frustrated with herself for not being able to openly express her feelings to her manager. Instead she kept quiet and brooded about the situation.

RUDE OR PREOCCUPIED?

Did the manager deliberately and rudely walk straight past her secretary? It is important always to step back and assess whether there could be another plausible explanation for a person's behaviour. Whatever the answer, the fact is we have control over **our own** emotions, thoughts and behaviour, not the other person's.

control over the other person

control over self

0%

100%

CBC can help a client reframe the way they think, feel and behave in a more positive way, even if the situation around them does not change. Furthermore, reframing helps to improve their emotional self-awareness not just of how they manage themselves, but also how they manage others around them.

We look next at the downside and upside of managing emotions in the workplace.

LOW EMOTIONAL INTELLIGENCE
DOWNSIDE

When a client's EI is **low**, this can be exhibited in the following ways:

- Poor impulse control – difficulty resisting an impulse to act, rage
- Difficulty managing stressful situations – clouded irrational thinking
- Interpersonal issues – blaming, judging and labelling others or themselves
- Lack of flexibility – black and white thinking, guided by rigid rules to making changes
- Irrational thinking – unable to view a situation the way it really is
- Poor emotional understanding – without self-awareness, how can they successfully manage other people's emotions

The knock on effect of unhealthy emotions surfacing in organisations is **low morale**, leading to:

- £millions lost in time spent recruiting new people, time off for stress, anxiety, drug abuse and depression related issues
- An under-performing organisation

HIGH EMOTIONAL INTELLIGENCE

UPSIDE

When a client's EI is **high**:

- Emotions and thinking are rational, balanced and healthy

- Decision making is not clouded by concealed emotions and negative thoughts that lead to unhelpful actions

- The individual is more adept at managing themselves and their relationships with others

CB coaches can help their clients develop healthy emotions at work by tackling and disabling unhelpful thoughts that activate or trigger an emotional response.

HIGH EMOTIONAL INTELLIGENCE

By raising a client's emotional self-awareness both **cognitive** (how they think, ie thoughts, feelings and beliefs) and **behavioural** (actions taken, eg a display of anger or impatience), you give them a basis upon which to build EI competencies including: nurturing relationships, managing emotional outbursts of anger, and learning to express the self in an assertive manner.

The more that individuals address the cognitive and behavioural aspects offered by CBC, the closer you come to the development of an emotionally intelligent organisation.

We look now at a case study featuring Matteo, an IT professional whose story runs throughout this pocketbook.

CASE STUDY

Matteo worked as a systems analyst for a large banking group in the city of London. His talents in his technical role were soon recognised and he was promoted to team leader managing a team of ten. Matteo had never actually managed people before, only a square box in front of him, which did not answer back! It soon became clear to his manager that his lack of people skills was creating a lot of tension within the team.

HR, after consultation with his manager, referred him to a coach. The coach wanted to help Matteo understand himself better as a way to nurture his people skills and improve his management of his team.

Before starting the coaching process, the coach wanted to get an EI baseline assessment on Matteo. This would make evident which EI competencies and skills needed to be worked on during the coaching intervention, and point out the weakest areas that needed development. He planned a further test in six months' time to evaluate the extent of any improvement in Matteo's EI. The coach selected the BarOn Emotional Quotient Inventory (EQ-i), a scientifically validated measure of social and emotional intelligence developed by Professor Reuven Bar-On in the 1980s.

CASE STUDY

These are the five scales used in the EQ-i to measure EI capabilities, competencies and skills:

Intrapersonal: measures the inner self – emotional self-awareness, self-regard, independence, assertiveness and self-actualisation.

Interpersonal: measures relationship skills – empathy, interpersonal skills and social responsibility.

Adaptability: measures how we assess and respond to situations – flexibility, reality testing and problem solving.

Stress management: measures the ability to handle stressful situations without falling apart – stress tolerance and impulse control.

General mood: measures the client's outlook on life – optimism and happiness.

Source: MHS Multi-health Systems Inc

CASE STUDY

Matteo's EQ-i scores revealed high emotional self-awareness; a good base for the coach to work from. His scores for flexibility, though, were low. One reason people have trouble with flexibility is that their irrational beliefs get in the way. In Matteo's case, his unrealistically high standards for himself and for others were causing him stress, leading him to display anger to colleagues and damaging his interpersonal relations with them.

Working together, Matteo and his coach drew up a plan of action for him:

- Look at his reactions to and judgements of particular incidents
- Improve his impulse control (impatience/anger) triggers linked to his thoughts and beliefs
- Improve his listening by social awareness training in interpersonal skills
- Develop strategies better to manage his own emotions and those of his colleagues, including appropriate assertiveness training
- Understand how his inflexibility and rigid demands for others to meet his standards led to his behaviour

The coach wanted to establish how Matteo's thoughts and beliefs were driving his emotional responses.

WHAT ARE AUTOMATIC THOUGHTS?

We look next at how thoughts and beliefs can hinder the change process – starting with automatic thoughts.

Thoughts and emotions feed off one another. For example, the more fearful, anxious or angry an individual becomes, the more distorted their thoughts. It makes sense, therefore, that before a client can change behaviours, they have to change what happens inside their minds – how they **think**, because this ultimately impacts how they **feel** and go on to **behave**, driven by their emotions.

Aaron Beck, a cognitive behavioural therapist (CBT), developed the cognitive model which has been used very successfully in cognitive behavioural therapy since the 1960s. Beck states that:

" *The interpretation of a situation, rather than the situation itself, often expressed in automatic thoughts, influences one's subsequent emotion, behaviour and physiological response.* "

(37)

AUTOMATIC THOUGHTS

The more distorted the thoughts are, the stronger the emotional reaction. Automatic thoughts don't knock politely at the door before waltzing in. Aaron Beck observed that his clients with depression had an *internal dialogue* of negative self-talk going on in their heads which inhibited them from thinking rationally. He sought to identify the unhealthy and unhelpful negative automatic thoughts (NATS) and replace them with more balanced ones. Here is an example of a negative automatic thought (NAT).

'I must be perfect in everything I do. If not I am a failure'.

AUTOMATIC THOUGHT
'*I am a failure.*'

The **ABCDE** model, which forms the centrepiece of the cognitive behavioural coaching approach, is a very useful tool for the coach to use in exploring unhelpful automatic thoughts. This is the subject of the next chapter.

ABCDE MODEL

Just because I think so
does not mean it is true.

CENTREPIECE OF CBC

The **ABCDE** model (see next page) is the centrepiece of cognitive behavioural coaching and is a useful tool to use with your client in exploring any moments of low emotional intelligence they may be experiencing. It is a 'stage model' to be worked through with a client, moving slowly through each stage and only after complete resolution moving on.

The model was pioneered by Albert Ellis, the founding father of Rational Emotive Behavioural Therapy (REBT).
He conducted his research and the application of rational emotive behavioural therapy from this premise:

> ❝We are disturbed not by events, but by the beliefs which we hold about them.❞
> **Epictetus**, the Greek Stoic philosopher.

The **ABCDE** model can also be used to examine Aaron Beck's negative automatic thoughts (NATS).

ABCDE MODEL

THE MODEL

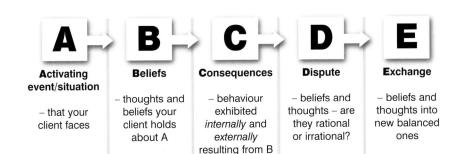

A	B	C	D	E
Activating event/situation	**Beliefs**	**Consequences**	**Dispute**	**Exchange**
– that your client faces	– thoughts and beliefs your client holds about A	– behaviour exhibited *internally* and *externally* resulting from B	– beliefs and thoughts – are they rational or irrational?	– beliefs and thoughts into new balanced ones

The ABCDE exercises that follow can be applied to any areas of your client's personal or professional life. We will be looking at the model slightly out of sequence, starting with A and then jumping to C.

41

ABCDE MODEL

 **ACTIVATING EVENT**

When something upsetting happens, all sorts of raw emotions, thoughts and feelings run around in your head. You have an internal conversation with yourself about how to judge and evaluate the event. The ABCDE model helps you to separate the emotions you feel from the event itself, revealing your thought and belief patterns and helping you to replace unhelpful ones with a more positive approach.

Check this exercise out for yourself.

Answer the following questions and write your responses down on a sheet of paper divided into columns ABCDE. You will need to allow plenty of room for detailed answers.

A = Activating event. Think of a recent situation that you felt frustrated and upset about. It is important to **be specific**. Eg: I had an argument with a work colleague.

Q1: What was the upsetting *situation*, known as the activating event or trigger?
Describe the actual event leading to the feelings of distress. Write it down in column A.

ABCDE MODEL

A ACTIVATING EVENT

EMOTIONS & THOUGHTS

Also write down in column A your unhelpful negative feelings and the unpleasant automatic thoughts that preceded them. Again be specific.

Q2. What were your emotions: did you feel angry, upset, anxious, tearful?

Q3. What were the automatic thought(s) that preceded the emotion(s): what was going through your mind just before you started to feel this way? Eg: '*I should not be spoken to in this way, I feel useless.*'

Having completed part A (the activating event/trigger) we now go straight to C (the consequences).

ABCDE MODEL

C CONSEQUENCES

Q4. What were your behaviours (internal and external) that accompanied the activating event? We are looking for the consequences of the powerful combination of thoughts and emotions you were feeling, eg:

- **Internally**: red mist rising, increased heart rate, butterflies in your stomach, clenched fists
- **Externally**: angry and upset, you storm out of the room

Write down what happened in column **C**:

Internally ....

Externally ....

Having completed parts A and C of the model, we move on to look at B (Beliefs) and D (Disputing them).

ABCDE MODEL

B BELIEFS

At this stage of the ABCDE model the coach can work with the client to help them understand that it is not the activating event (A) that leads to the consequences (C), but their **beliefs** (B) that **trigger** the negative **automatic thoughts**.

Beliefs are how an individual thinks and perceives a situation to be. It is their view of the world, as they see it and know it to be true, learnt from childhood experiences. If these beliefs are *irrational* rather than *rational*, they act as a **trigger** in producing recurring negative automatic thoughts. For example:

BELIEF: Everything I do must be perfect. If not, I am a failure.
AUTOMATIC THOUGHT: I am a failure.

Such rigid views and rules, particularly when unhelpful and distorted, generate high levels of stress and anxiety at the thought of failing. But the demand is impossible to achieve – no one is **perfect**.

We look next at how to Dispute (D) Beliefs and Automatic Thoughts (B).

D DISPUTING THE BELIEF

The statements on the following pages are based on the work of David Burns who, from his research, put together ten common thinking styles that he refers to as **cognitive distortions**. The distortions act to trigger recurring negative automatic thoughts and beliefs.

The statements that follow describe very common thinking distortions. We all fall into some of them from time to time, and each of us will have our 'favourites'. When working with your clients you can help them identify their regular patterns.

For the purposes of the exercise, now read through the ten statements to see if you have used any of these styles in your activating incident. Then, using the examples provided under the **D**, start **Disputing** them. Are they really true?

ABCDE MODEL

TEN COMMON THINKING DISTORTIONS

1. OVER-GENERALISING

You come to a general conclusion based on a single event or one piece of evidence. If something bad happens once, you expect it to happen again and again. Such thoughts often include the words 'always' and 'never'.

Examples of over-generalising are:

- I forgot to finish that project on time. I never do things right
- He did not want to go out with me. I will always be alone
- I always make mistakes
- Everyone thinks I am stupid

Catch yourself over-generalising

DISPUTE

Ask: where is the evidence?

- Am I over-generalising?
- Where are the facts to support my thinking, based on a single incident?

You are taking your feelings from one situation and projecting them onto other situations in an equally negative way.

TEN COMMON THINKING DISTORTIONS

2. FILTERING

When you filter you focus solely on the negative aspects of a situation, and ignore or dismiss all the positive aspects – the things that went right.

An example of filtering is:

- I know my boss said most of my report was excellent, but he also said there were a number of mistakes that had to be corrected – he must think I'm really hopeless

Consider the whole picture

DISPUTE

Ask: where is the evidence?

- Am I looking at the negatives, while ignoring the positives?
- Is there a more balanced way to look at this?

Count up your negatives versus your positives – for every negative event place a positive against it.

TEN COMMON THINKING DISTORTIONS

3. MAGNIFYING

Do you sometimes find yourself fearing the worst and fretting about it to the point of turning it into a catastrophe? Or exaggerating a situation to look worse than it actually is?

Examples of magnifying are:

- This is awful. I'll make a complete fool of myself and people will laugh at me
- There's that look from the boss again. I just know I am going to be sacked

DISPUTE
- What is the worst thing that can happen?
- Will this matter in one year's time?
- What is the best thing that can happen?
- Is there anything good about the situation?
- What is most likely to happen?
- Is there any other way of viewing this situation?

Strike a realistic balance between optimism and pessimism

When things go wrong, try to avoid turning a molehill into a mountain. Search for the evidence: How awful is it really? Is it so terrible?

49

TEN COMMON THINKING DISTORTIONS

4. ALL OR NOTHING THINKING

You think in black and white terms: things are right or wrong, good or bad. There is no middle ground.

Examples of all or nothing thinking are:

- If I fall short of perfection I am a complete failure
- If I lose a customer, my business will collapse
- Everyone must like me, or else I am a total failure

DISPUTE

Ask: where is the evidence?

- Is it really so bad, or am I seeing things in black and white?
- What other way is there to think about this situation?
- Am I taking an extreme view?

Look for shades of grey and bright colours

It is important to avoid thinking about things in terms of extremes. Just because something is not completely perfect does not mean that it is a complete write-off. Don't beat yourself up when you make a slight error. Nobody is perfect.

TEN COMMON THINKING DISTORTIONS

5. DISQUALIFYING THE POSITIVE

This is another example of a mental filter. You reject positive experiences by denying them and insisting they don't count.

Examples of discounting the positive are:

Celebrate your successes

- The person who does a good job, but thinks it wasn't good enough or that anyone else could have done just as well
- The trainer who receives 20 positive evaluations from the workshop participants, and only notices the three negatives

DISPUTE

Say to yourself:

- Discounting the positive takes the joy out of my life and makes me feel inadequate
- Discounting the positive only leaves one option, accepting the negative, which is of course not at all helpful

Try to remind yourself that filtering out good experiences only drags you down.

TEN COMMON THINKING DISTORTIONS
6. JUMPING TO THE WRONG CONCLUSIONS

This distortion is about making negative interpretations of other people's thoughts, feelings and behaviours without any actual facts to support your conclusion.

Examples of jumping to the wrong conclusions are:

- **Mind reading**: Thinking that people are thinking badly of you. '*I can tell she secretly hates me, because she did not say hello to me*'
- **Fortune telling**: '*I just know something awful is going to happen*'

DISPUTE
- Where is the evidence? How do you know what other people are thinking or that something awful is going to happen?

Just because an individual assumes something, does that mean it is right? Search for hard facts to support the assumption.

As the old adage goes, don't judge a book by its cover

TEN COMMON THINKING DISTORTIONS

7. LABELLING

When someone uses labelling, they call themselves (or other people) names.

Examples of labelling are:

- I am a loser
- I am boring
- She is an idiot
- He is a creep

DISPUTE

- Where is the evidence to support that these labels are correct?
- Are these labels preventing you from seeing other aspects of people?
- Can you label a specific **situation** instead of labelling yourself or others?

How would you do this?

> 'Once you label me you negate me.'
> Soren Kierkegaard

53

TEN COMMON THINKING DISTORTIONS

8. EMOTIONAL REASONING

This involves using your emotions as proof that things are the way that they are: *I feel it, so it must be true*. Feelings are treated as facts.

Examples of emotional reasoning are:

- I feel stupid and boring, so I must be stupid and boring
- We didn't get the order because I know they don't like me

DISPUTE

- Where is the evidence for your assumptions and intuitions?

Write a list of alternative explanations

54

TEN COMMON THINKING DISTORTIONS

9. SHOULDS & MUSTS

Using 'should' or 'must' statements – for yourself and others – can set up unrealistic expectations. It means operating by rigid rules and allowing no room for flexibility; having ideas that things can only be done one way.

Example of should and musts:

- People must always be polite
- I should not get angry – people should be nice to me all the time
- I must always be on time
- I must always be perfect at everything I do

DISPUTE

The world is not set in stone. It would be nice if people were always polite, did not get angry and arrived on time but it is unrealistic to expect it every time. Using 'should' or 'must' statements leads to anguish when the rule or demand is not met.

Don't be too hard on yourself

TEN COMMON THINKING DISTORTIONS

10. PERSONALISATION & BLAME

Personalisation means assuming personal responsibility for an event, regardless of your actual impact on it. It leads to guilt, shame, and feelings of inadequacy.

Examples of personalisation and blame are:

- Thinking that what people say or do is some kind of reaction to you, or is in some way related to you (*they must be talking about me*)
- Blaming yourself for a problem that may not even be in your control (*it is all my fault*) and consequently feeling guilty and worthless

Or • Blaming the other person and denying your own role in the problem (*it is all your fault*)

DISPUTE

- Are you really to blame? Is this all about you? Where is the evidence?
- What other explanations are there for this situation?

Try not to blame yourself unjustifiably for others' failures. Consider that there are many causes contributing to each outcome, before drawing a conclusion.

> 'Common sense is the collection of prejudices acquired by age eighteen.'
> Albert Einstein

56

USING SOCRATIC QUESTIONS

Once you have worked with your client to identify the types of thinking they are using in a particular situation, you can use Socratic questioning to explore the reality. Socratic questioning originates from the Greek philosopher Socrates. The process involves the coach asking a series of questions in order to explore the reality of the situation, rather than a distorted version of it.

It encourages your client to look at the **evidence** for their unhelpful thoughts and/or limiting beliefs.

This questioning approach helps the client move from their current position towards more helpful thoughts and actions, by replacing old negative thoughts and developing more positive thoughts that are:

Realistic

Constructive

In perspective

ABCDE MODEL

USING SOCRATIC QUESTIONS

Some examples of Socratic questions have already been provided within the ten most common thinking styles. Here are some more:

- What was going through your mind before you started to feel this way?
- What images or memories do you have of this situation?
- What would you say to someone else in this situation?
- Are you using unhelpful thinking styles, eg all or nothing thinking or labelling?
- What would be a better way of looking at this?
- What other thinking can you adopt now you have the evidence that your thinking is unhelpful?

Socratic questions help to raise your client's self-awareness and can be adapted to fit whatever situation you are both working on. The coach can guide the client to learn how to start disputing their own beliefs and automatic thoughts around the activating event.

On the following page, see for yourself which common thinking styles Matteo is using.

SELF-AWARENESS
CASE STUDY: MATTEO'S THOUGHTS

Paul is an idiot and I have told him so – he never does anything right in my eyes. Loser!

Some team members do not come up to my standards. They must do it my way or it won't work.

I cannot trust certain team members to do anything right, the way I want it to be. This is why I get stressed and lose my temper, even over small things now.

SELF-AWARENESS
CASE STUDY: MATTEO'S THOUGHTS

In these statements, all uttered during a coaching session, the coach picked up that Matteo was using **labelling** (Paul was an idiot); **'must' statements** (his rigid rules based on his own extreme standards of perfection), and **filtering** (only commenting on the negative aspect of his team members' performance, and ignoring any positives).

He was adopting a pessimistic, judgemental and perfectionist viewpoint. The coach helped him analyse whether these views were irrational or unhelpful to him in managing the situation.

A good coach is used to *attuning their ears*, actively listening out for any unhelpful negative thinking styles the client may be using when describing the situation they are being coached for, eg better communications skills, anger, assertiveness or stress.

E EXCHANGE NEGATIVE BELIEFS & THOUGHTS

❝Taking a new step, uttering a new word is what people fear most.❞

Fyodor Dostoevsky,
Russian novelist

*❝Long established habits like having a short temper or being a perfectionist, are deeply ingrained. In such cases, the client needs to work both at **unlearning** the old, automatic habit and at **replacing** it with the new improved one.❞*

Daniel Goleman

ABCDE MODEL

E EXCHANGE NEGATIVE BELIEFS & THOUGHTS

Having covered the first four parts of the ABCDE model, we now look in detail at **E** – how to **Exchange** negative unhelpful beliefs and thoughts for new more balanced ones.

In order to sustain real and lasting change, a client needs to be motivated to change unhelpful thinking patterns in the way they **think, feel and behave** and to set up an environment that will support them in making such changes and lead them towards goal attainment.

The goal should be **practised, rehearsed and relived everyday** in order to keep it at the front of conscious awareness and give it sufficient focus to make it absolutely specific.

The key: there is no getting away from it, persistent rehearsal and practice of new behaviours is essential to unlock the door of real behaviour change. Keeping a thoughts journal is an excellent way to move forward.

ABCDE MODEL

E EXCHANGE NEGATIVE BELIEFS & THOUGHTS
KEEPING A THOUGHTS JOURNAL

A thoughts journal is a useful tool to get your clients to record how their thoughts affect how they feel and react in situations. It helps them to **capture** and **identify** automatic thoughts and irrational thinking that are acting as blocks to moving forward.

Once your client is in the habit of disputing their negative self-talk, they will find it easier to handle difficult situations and, as a result, will feel less stressed, more confident and in better control of their emotions.

We look next at using positive self-talk to help **exchange** (**E**) and stamp out negative self-talk.

E EXCHANGE NEGATIVE BELIEFS & THOUGHTS

BALANCED SELF-TALK

The research that has been conducted into the importance of positive self-talk has proved encouraging for the effective transfer of learning.

- Balanced self-talk is a coping strategy your client can use that will help them to break the vicious cycle of negative self-talk and focus on **positive self-talk** instead

- It takes practice, but the goal is well worth achieving – replacing nagging self-defeating thoughts with positive energising self-talk

The Balancing Thoughts sheet on the following page gives you a format to use to encourage regular practice.

ABCDE MODEL

E EXCHANGE NEGATIVE BELIEFS & THOUGHTS

BALANCED SELF-TALK

Ask your client to write, in the left-hand column, a negative thought or situation that they are dealing with at present. In the right-hand column they should write down an alternative statement that balances the negative one by moderating it in a realistic manner or by giving it a simple positive ending.

Balancing Thoughts sheet

Negative thought/belief	change to	Realistic balancing statement
If my presentation doesn't go as planned, I am useless and can't do anything right.	▷	I plan to prepare and practise for the presentation. If I fluff a line it is not the end of the world.
I've got to criticise my employees' ideas.	▷	I will offer supportive ideas.
I must demand a review meeting.	▷	I will ask my employee for feedback when ready.
I am a failure if I get this wrong.	▷	I have done a lot of good work in the past; if I make a mistake it doesn't mean I'm a failure.

ABCDE MODEL

E EXCHANGE NEGATIVE BELIEFS & THOUGHTS

BALANCED SELF-TALK

Ask your client to **catch** themselves if they feel the recurring negative thoughts and irrational thinking creeping up on them. They need to refer to the positive Balancing Thoughts statement and repeat it to themselves in order to focus their thoughts and create a more positive frame of mind. Just doing this should make them feel more in control and less anxious or stressed.

The key: practise counter-balancing your thoughts by using positive self-talk to dispute the negative thinking.

Next we will look at a visualisation technique, another way of replacing negative thoughts with more realistic ones. Returning to our friend Matteo, we start by looking at his Balancing Thoughts sheet.

ABCDE MODEL

E EXCHANGE NEGATIVE BELIEFS & THOUGHTS

BALANCED SELF-TALK

Matteo's goal was:

> *To improve the quality of my relationship with my team*

Below is his list of negative thoughts and counter-balancing positive thoughts:

Negative thought	change to	Realistic balancing statement
I must challenge my team.	▷	I will fully discuss my team's ideas.
I am right and she is definitely wrong.	▷	I can listen to the other team member's point of view.
I only see what they've done wrong.	▷	I notice both the positives and the negatives.

After producing his list, Matteo was asked to do a visualisation exercise.

ABCDE MODEL

E EXCHANGE NEGATIVE BELIEFS & THOUGHTS

VISUALISATION TECHNIQUES

Visualisation techniques are a powerful way to keep focused. These are the steps:

- Sit in a chair and repeat the positive list from your Balancing Thoughts sheet. (Pin it up on the wall or record it on a tape recorder)
- Mentally rehearse it
- Visualise what you will be able to see, eg the meeting room, the faces of your team when you are working with them on these new ideas
- Imagine the conversation, the words used; hear yourself saying them
- Imagine now how you are feeling as the relationships improve and members of your team begin to trust you more
- Imagine now how much more confident your team members are becoming
- Think what the long-term feeling would be

ABCDE MODEL

E EXCHANGE NEGATIVE BELIEFS & THOUGHTS

MORNING MINDFULNESS

Another technique CB coaches find effective is **morning mindfulness**.

When you wake up in the morning, put yourself in the frame of mind you wish to be in throughout the day, in terms of your thoughts and behaviour.

- How you will act with others
- Your feelings
- Your thoughts
- Your emotions all working in unison

Taking the time to do this helps people to start the day in a good frame of mind and face any challenges ahead. Some clients choose to do yoga or meditation: any exercise that helps the mind become clear of unhelpful negative thinking styles is good.

ABCDE MODEL

E EXCHANGE NEGATIVE BELIEFS & THOUGHTS

ENACTING NEW BEHAVIOURS

From identifying negatives, balancing them with positives and using visualisation, we now move to **enacting** the new behaviour. The likelihood of successful habit change can be assessed by the ease or difficulty with which a client can do this. Until the behaviours are put into daily practice in a forceful persistent manner (rather than on an intermittent basis), no real change will take place.

Returning to Matteo, his challenge was to change from a telling approach to one of listening, and to ask questions and stay calm instead of immediately giving his own opinion and taking control in a reactive situation. His coach chose to use the following strategies.

ABCDE MODEL

E EXCHANGE NEGATIVE BELIEFS & THOUGHTS

ENACTING NEW BEHAVIOURS

- **Role play** – they acted out different scenarios to prepare him for the situation, looking to develop appropriate assertiveness skills, so that he could put his point across in a non-confrontational way without indulging in blaming, judging, or issuing 'must' statements

- **Planning** – he worked on developing supportive, positive, balanced thoughts before entering the room

- **Active listening** – using this encourages openness and co-operation because the other person knows they have been heard

- **Modelling** – Matteo was told to find a person he admired who managed people well, and talk to them about their experiences and observe how they talked and interacted with others. Managers and leaders with high EI have these competencies and skills

- **Homework assignments** – Matteo was given plenty of opportunity for reflection and analysis of his behaviour

ABCDE MODEL

E EXCHANGE NEGATIVE BELIEFS & THOUGHTS
HOMEWORK ASSIGNMENTS

Homework assignments are an integral part of cognitive behavioural coaching. You might ask the client to analyse and reflect on particular situations and record them in their thoughts journal, or to try out specific actions to see what works for them and what doesn't.

In reviewing the client's task assignments, the following questions are useful:

- What did you learn? (*Review the ABCDE thoughts journal with them*)
- What do you think you should continue to do for your homework assignment – what is working for you?
- Can you think of previous situations in your life when the cognitive behavioural approach would have helped you?
- How will you remember to use the cognitive behavioural coaching tools next time?
- What positive things happened during the week?
- Did any problems come up? If so, how well did you handle them? If the problem happened again, how would you handle it next time?

ABCDE MODEL

E EXCHANGE NEGATIVE BELIEFS & THOUGHTS

HOMEWORK ASSIGNMENTS

You will find plenty of occasions when the client has not completed the homework assignments. There could be many different reasons for this:

- The client may be struggling in some way
- Just not motivated
- Their belief in their ability to succeed in making such changes is acting as an obstacle
- They are finding the changes uncomfortable

It is important to support your client in any obstacles they may be facing in completing the homework assignments. During the next coaching session the coach will begin to get a real idea of the client's situation. On the following page are some sample questions you may find useful to establish the nature of the problem.

ABCDE MODEL

E EXCHANGE NEGATIVE BELIEFS & THOUGHTS

HOMEWORK ASSIGNMENTS

If the client did not do the set homework assignment(s):

- What got in the way?
- Were there practical problems?
- Were there automatic thoughts?
- What can the client do to make it more likely they will do their homework assignment next time?

We have covered just a few examples of the various techniques you can adopt to bring about part E of the ABCDE model. Further reading is detailed at the end of this pocketbook.

Success is down to the motivation of the client, with the coach's support, to use the techniques and to incorporate them by constant practice until the new emotions, feelings, thoughts, beliefs and behaviours are embedded. Practice of homework assignments becomes an essential part of building solid foundations for change.

COACH'S TOOLBOX

INTRODUCTION

In this chapter we look at the importance of you, as coach, being aware of the dynamics of change and of the different levels of your client's **motivation to make changes**, ie in the way they think, feel and behave.

Following this we will go on to explore the importance of setting **goals** and the appropriate structures that need to be put in place for effective behaviour change to take place.

We begin with the Transtheoretical Model of behaviour change (TTM), a model you can use to explain a client's patterns of behaviour and explore how ready/committed they are to the change process.

COACH'S TOOLBOX

BEHAVIOUR CHANGE MODEL

The Transtheoretical Model of behaviour change (TTM), or as it is more commonly known, the Stages of Change model (SOC) was originally developed in the late 1970s and early 1980s by James Prochaska and Carlo DiClemente at the University of Rhode Island in the United States. It suggests that behaviour change happens in six separate stages:

Pre-contemplation – not yet acknowledging there is a problem in their behaviour that needs to be changed

Contemplation – experiences motivation to change and motivation not to change (ambivalence)

Determination – getting ready to change

Action – is motivated and actively practising the new behaviours

Maintenance – keeps going at a steady pace

Relapse – returns to old behaviour and abandons new changes

BEHAVIOUR CHANGE MODEL

RELAPSE

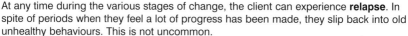

At any time during the various stages of change, the client can experience **relapse**. In spite of periods when they feel a lot of progress has been made, they slip back into old unhealthy behaviours. This is not uncommon.

The role of the coach here is to support the client in building confidence to face what can be a challenging prospect. You need to monitor progress through the various stages of change, encouraging practice of the new behaviours until the old, unhealthy ones have been eliminated and the client reaches the exit door with the new behaviours firmly embedded.

BEHAVIOUR CHANGE MODEL
CYCLE OF CHANGE

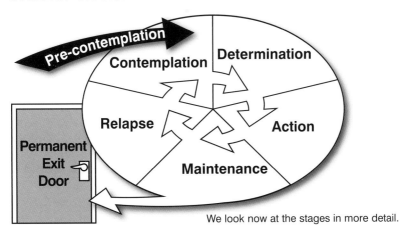

We look now at the stages in more detail.

COACH'S TOOLBOX

GAUGING STAGES OF CHANGE

The implication of the TTM model is that clients at different stages are likely to benefit from different interventions. The authors state that '*the processes of change within this model are distinct and measurable and that efficient self change depends on doing the right things (processes) at the right time (stages)*'. To bring the model to life and maximise the chances of successful behavioural change, a coach may wish to integrate the Motivational Interviewing approach developed by Miller and Rollnick in the early 1990s.

As a coach you will already be using the principles of:

- Expressing empathy – use skilful reflective listening without judging or criticising

- Developing discrepancy – help the client recognise the discrepancy between their behaviour and their personal goals without feeling they are being pressurised

- Rolling with resistance – do not fight any resistance, eg with a client who blames, challenges or plays down a negative situation

- Supporting efficacy – build their confidence and ability to succeed in making changes

On the following pages, drawing from Miller and Rollnick's approach, are stage specific coaching tactics for facilitating change.

COACH'S TOOLBOX

STAGE SPECIFIC COACHING TACTICS

Pre-contemplation: not yet acknowledging there is a problem

As demonstrated in Matteo's case study, the use of self-awareness assessments (eg behavioural and 360 multi-rater feedback tools) is an effective coaching intervention to gauge the emotional intelligence of your client before and after the coaching process, to establish what low EI factors may be holding them back.

Self-awareness assessments can also provide the breakthrough with a client experiencing difficulties in seeing why they need to change at all. Here are some examples of resistance you may already be familiar with:

- That's just the way I am, I will never change, I got this from my mother/father
- I don't cause my own feelings – the other person is to blame for starting this
- It will be difficult and uncomfortable
- I might fail or make mistakes
- I can't be bothered
- I don't see this as a problem

STAGE SPECIFIC COACHING TACTICS

Contemplation: unsure about it (ambivalence)

If a client is at the contemplation stage, two opposing thoughts are at play. Consider, for example, an individual who knows smoking is bad for them, and yet carries on doing it. You can describe this stage as sitting on the fence.

At the contemplation stage it is useful to work with the client to increase resilience and confidence in the face of uncomfortable changes. You can also explore together the **pros** and **cons** of making a behaviour change.

Check out the decisional balance sheet on the following page.

82

STAGE SPECIFIC COACHING TACTICS

The pros and cons combine to form a balance sheet of comparative potential gains and losses. In doing so the client's awareness is raised about the costs and benefits of changing, and how things could be better.

Decisional Balance Sheet

The Pros (Of making a change)	The Cons (Of making a change)
What do I gain from…?	**What do I lose from…?**
What would I gain if I stopped…?	**What would I lose if I stopped…?**

Source: adapted from Janis and Mann (1977)

You can also use this tool in the pre-contemplation stage, and to track ambivalence throughout the other stages, to gauge whether the scales are still tipped in favour of making the change and the client remains motivated and committed.

STAGE SPECIFIC COACHING TACTICS

Determination: ready for change

If your client is at the determination stage of the behaviour change model, here are some useful pointers:

- Help your client to focus on the future, working on a clear vision and action steps that will move them towards their goals

- Continue to build self-efficacy in their ability to work successfully towards behaviour change

- Negotiate goals with them, letting the client decide, but ensuring that the goals are specific, measurable, attainable, realistic and time-framed (SMART)

- Explore the skills or information they require to reach the goal

STAGE SPECIFIC COACHING TACTICS

Action: motivated and actively practising the new behaviour/s

Once your client reaches the action stage, encourage small steps forward, monitor progress and move towards setting more stretching goals. They can do this by undertaking task assignments and putting things into practice.

Here are some useful pointers to work with when a client is at this stage of change:

- Introduce CBC homework assignments
- Develop and agree an action plan
- Get agreement and a statement of commitment of action from your client
- Continue to assess readiness for change
- Encourage small steps
- Empower the client

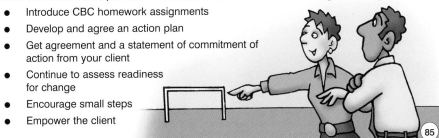

STAGE SPECIFIC COACHING TACTICS

Maintenance: keeps going at a steady pace

Now you need to help your client to identify and use
strategies to prevent relapse. The maintenance stage
involves supporting their progress by keeping a
check on how they are coming along in the
change process. For example, are they:

- Still tracking their thoughts by
  completing the thoughts journal
  every day?

- Actively disputing any unhelpful
  thoughts and replacing them with
  more balanced thoughts?

- Practising the new behaviours at a
  steady daily pace?

COACH'S TOOLBOX

STAGE SPECIFIC COACHING TACTICS

Relapse

If, as commonly happens, the client relapses, your job is to help them to renew the process of contemplation, determination and action without feeling too stuck or demoralised. Nobody is perfect! Relapse is disappointing, and can leave people wanting to give up completely. It is extremely common until the new behaviour is firmly cemented in the psyche. The following guidelines will be useful for this stage:

- Reframe relapse as **a normal part** of the change process
- Rebuild any confidence knocks
- Minimise embarrassment, shame and guilt
- Look for past successes and build on them
- Try something new
- Accept that leaving the comfort zone can always be difficult and use this to strengthen the client's determination

NB Tread carefully. Mentioning relapse too early in the process, eg at pre-contemplation stage, can give people the excuse not to try.

MOTIVATION TO CHANGE
CASE STUDY

We now continue with Matteo's story.

After providing him with the feedback from his EQ-i results, and prior to taking him through the ABCDE model, the coach wanted to establish how motivated Matteo was to start working on his own development, both cognitively and behaviourally.

Using the Decisional Balance Sheet to gain further insight and to gauge Matteo's readiness for change, the coach explored with him **what he had to gain** versus **what he would lose** in making the changes.

This produced a light bulb moment for Matteo. He finally realised that his own performance in his role of team leader might be adversely affected by his current behaviour.

We look next at the importance of having the correct structure in place when your client is setting their goal(s).

SETTING GOALS – THE RESEARCH

Research on goal setting and performance at work found that the: *'CBC coaching approach was the most powerful in enhancing performance and goal attainment, as well as enhancing self-regulation, self-concept, and general well being'*. (Grant 2003)

Similar evidence-based coaching studies found that the cognitive behavioural coaching psychology approach *'increased performance and decreased stress and depression at work'*. (Grant and Green 2001)

Edwin Locke, the distinguished American psychologist, reviewed the research into goal setting and performance at work. He stated that: *'Outcome goals that are difficult and specifically and explicitly defined allow performance to be precisely regulated and lead to high performance'*. (Locke 1996)

Locke and Latham (1990) concluded that, **'goal setting increases performance from 10 percent to 30 percent'.**

Coaching programmes usually adopt the SMART model of goal setting, helpful in ensuring that goals stay realistic.

COACH'S TOOLBOX

SMART GOALS

Let's return to Matteo, whose goal is: To improve my relationship with my team within the next two months.

Specific – the goal is clearly defined, not vague

Measurable – it can be monitored and measured by the EQ-i (emotional intelligence quotient), with 360 multi-rater feedback from his manager, team members, and others who know him (pre and post, ie after six months) and there will be positive feedback from others in between

Attainable – he is motivated to pursue it and it is within his capability

Realistic – it is not out of reach; he will be taking small steps to start with

Time framed – there is an adequate time frame (which could be divided into short, medium and long-term goals so that a careful check can be made on progress – this helps motivation)

90

SMART GOALS

THE HOUSE OF CHANGE

Before SMART goals are set in place it is important that the client has a **vision** of where they want to be. It is no good saying my *vision* is: 'To improve my interpersonal skills', or 'To become more assertive' if you take no action to achieve the desired goal.

One of the reasons that individuals fail in their change efforts is that they only focus on what they have to **do** differently, ie changing the behaviour aspect of the situation without bringing into the equation the thoughts, feelings and emotions that are required to accompany behaviour change.

In designing a vision of the future, the House of Change model developed by Anthony Grant (see reading list, page 110) is a great way to guide a client towards identifying specific goal/s and turning them into SMART goals. On the following page is the house of change structure for supporting change. To sustain real and lasting change all the structures need to be in place.

SMART GOALS
THE HOUSE OF CHANGE

'In order for positive change to take place effectively and for goals to be reached successfully, it is important that the house of change, as illustrated below, has four sturdy corners, each interacting with the other.' (Grant 2001)

It doesn't work just to address two corners of the house: *Situation* (the support mechanisms in place in making changes) and *Behaviour* (the consequences of an individual's actions), and forget about the cognitive aspects of *Thoughts* and *Emotions*. All four corners of the house need addressing simultaneously. If the four corners that support the structure are not firmly in place, then the house will collapse.

We now return to Matteo to look in more detail at using the house of change.

SMART GOALS
USING THE HOUSE OF CHANGE

The coach asked Matteo to visualise his goal, make it SMART and state it with **power** and **conviction**.

Goal: I am going to improve the quality of my relationship with my team within the next two months.

Behaviour: *I would be doing…..* listening, supporting my team by giving positive feedback and encouragement.

Thoughts: *I would be thinking…..* I am going to take on board new knowledge, skills and techniques and improve my interpersonal skills.

SMART GOALS
USING THE HOUSE OF CHANGE

Emotions: *I would be feeling…..* excited and stimulated by the new challenge, improving self-efficacy and widening horizons for future promotion to manager of the IT department.

Situation: *I would have this situation…..* able to devote time to working on my interpersonal skills. My manager, HR and others around me are supportive.

Adapted from Anthony Grant 2001

Matteo then worked with his coach to put together a realistic workable action plan.

SIX CBC TIPS

1. **Start small:** keep it realistic by checking that the client is not taking on more than they can handle. First steps could be something like listening more to others, taking on an activity to reduce stress or depression, or changing their normally abrupt emails that offend others to ones that are short but polite.

2. **Affirmations:** are positive words and statements the client writes about themselves in the present tense. ('*I listen to what other people have to say.*') If used repetitively they can help build confidence and change a belief, or thoughts or feelings. They can be recorded on an audio tape, printed onto cards, typed onto a screen saver, put on the fridge or anywhere they can be seen regularly. You can also add pictures.

SIX CBC TIPS

3. **Write it down:** research shows that only 3 to 5% of individuals write down their goals. Suggest that they write a letter, addressed to themselves in the future, describing what they wish to be like. This helps move through the change process.

4. **Inform others/gain support:** suggest that your client lets others know what they intend to do. This can act as a powerful motivational driver and safety net.

5. **Weekly/fortnightly action plan:** agree to review developments with your client and adapt plans as necessary. Change what is not working and try something new.

6. **Practice makes perfect:** regular daily practice is the best way for new behaviours to become embedded.

EVALUATION OF
<u>EFFECTIVENESS</u>

INTRODUCTION

As coaching becomes more and more universally available, questions are being asked about how effective it actually is.

A survey conducted into coaching by the CIPD in 2009 highlighted evaluation of coaching practice as a particularly hot topic, stating that: *'the absence of systematic evaluation could be taken as evidence of the absence of coaching'*.

If coaching is to remain a valid intervention, organisations need to prove its lasting value in relation to its return on investment (ROI), but also more broadly in relation to its *'demonstrated value'*. (Anthony Grant)

Recent research studies have measured the effectiveness of adopting cognitive behavioural coaching interventions in the workplace. We will be looking at three of these studies.

EVALUATION OF EFFECTIVENESS

THREE CBC RESEARCH STUDIES

STUDY 1

1. Short-term cognitive behavioural coaching interventions: worth the effort or a waste of time? (Fiona Beddoes-Jones & Julia Miller, 2007)

This research study was conducted over three months with eight individuals taking part – a mixture of managers and leaders. The gist of the findings from the statistical analysis reported that:

> CBC interventions are effective and add significant and professional value for the eight individuals being coached. The overall impact was heightened self-awareness (the building block of emotional intelligence) and confidence.

Here is some anecdotal feedback from the participants to support the findings:

- *'This short-term coaching has been valuable to me'*
- *'My performance at work improved because of this coaching'*
- *'My colleagues have noticed a difference in the way I communicate and present myself'*

EVALUATION OF EFFECTIVENESS

THREE CBC RESEARCH STUDIES
STUDY 2

2. Outcomes for seven housing officers (Margaret Chapman, 2003)

This study was conducted over six months, involving five workshops and the practice of CBC techniques when not attending workshops. The intention of this piece of research was to look at the impact of cognitive behavioural coaching on team emotional intelligence.

The CB strategies used included:

- Creating a vision for the future and setting SMART goals
- Reframing using the ABCDE model
- Self-monitoring, ie identifying thinking patterns of negative self-talk
- Individual EI assessment, using the Boston EQ as an underlying measurement for pre and post statistical evaluation
- Recording of incidents arising at work in a personal journal

EVALUATION OF EFFECTIVENESS

THREE CBC RESEARCH STUDIES

STUDY 2 – FINDINGS

Of the five dimensions tested, see graph below, differences between pre and post measures were statistically significant in four. The exception was emotion management. As with Study 1, clients reported that **self-awareness** was the most significant gain. Again this indicates that using CB measures can improve a client's overall emotional intelligence.

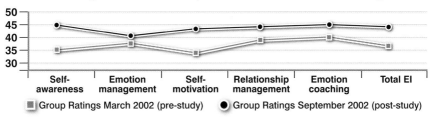

■ Group Ratings March 2002 (pre-study)   ● Group Ratings September 2002 (post-study)

*'The cognitive orientation of coaching enabled the individuals to **tilt their worlds** slightly and identify the relationship between their thoughts, feelings and behaviours.'* M. Chapman

Adapted from Chapman, M.A. (2004), Our Future in Focus. A case study of developing team emotional intelligence in the public sector.

EVALUATION OF EFFECTIVENESS

THREE CBC RESEARCH STUDIES

STUDY 3

3. Coaching for enhanced performance: comparing cognitive and behavioural approaches to coaching (Anthony Grant, 2006)

Our final research project is a series of three studies conducted with trainee accountants. This series included the following components:
● Research study a) *Behavioural coaching* (doing)
● Research study b) *Cognitive coaching* (thinking about how we think)
● Research study c) *Combined cognitive behavioural coaching*

The aim of the studies was to examine the impact of the three types of coaching approaches on trainee accountants:
● Their study-related goal attainment
● Their ability to self-regulate their emotions and behaviours
● Their ability to self-reflect and develop insight

The added benefit of this would be less anxiety and depression and an increase in overall well-being.

EVALUATION OF EFFECTIVENESS

THREE CBC RESEARCH STUDIES

STUDY 3

Each group of trainee accountants received 17 hours of programme time, over six separate sessions. The first session was a seven hour seminar with five two-hour follow-up workshops. A control group received no individual coaching and only completed the pre and post questionnaires.

The research study was again evaluated after one semester to see if any lasting changes had occurred.

The study centred on the House of Change model (see page 92). It involved looking at what the effects would be if only some of the four structures were in place, ie would the house fall down?

We will look at each of the three studies in turn, starting with the **behavioural only** coaching intervention.

EVALUATION OF EFFECTIVENESS

THREE CBC RESEARCH STUDIES
STUDY 3

The trainee accountants coached only on **behavioural aspects**, with no cognitive input, were taught to:

- Set SMART goals for academic study and monitor study-related behaviour

- Use the Transtheoretical Model focusing on behaviour rather than cognitive aspects

- Monitor study-related behaviour/s

- Use a log book setting out explicit goals for each study session

- Self-regulate their understanding of the coursework material

- Use environmental visual aids

- Use cues in the environment to remind them of their goals and study plans

EVALUATION OF EFFECTIVENESS

THREE CBC RESEARCH STUDIES

STUDY 3

Graph 1 shows the results for the **behavioural** group. In comparison with the control group, they improved significantly on their academic performance and showed reduced test anxiety. There was, however, little impact on self-regulation, ie managing their emotions and thoughts.

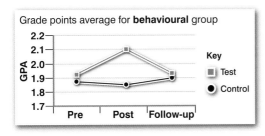

Grade points average for **behavioural** group

Key
- Test
- Control

The positive results from graph 1 were measured again after one semester to see if there had been any change. This time around there was a decline in academic performance.

EVALUATION OF EFFECTIVENESS

THREE CBC RESEARCH STUDIES
STUDY 3

The second group of trainees were coached only in the **cognitive aspects**, working on how to:

- Set SMART goals
- Understand the cycle of change
- Use self-talk and thought journals

- Learn to monitor, evaluate and restructure their emotions and cognitions

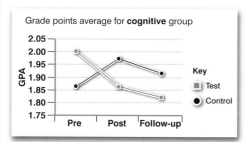

Grade points average for **cognitive** group

Key
- Test
- Control

There were significant changes in how the trainee accountants saw themselves. However, contrary to the behavioural only study, the cognitive only element was not enough to increase their academic performance. In fact it was the reverse, suggesting that it may be detrimental to use only the cognitive aspect. Furthermore, when conducting the follow up study one semester later, no significant differences were found between the cognitive study trainees and the control group.

THREE CBC RESEARCH STUDIES

STUDY 3

In the final group the trainees were taught both **cognitive** and **behavioural aspects**.

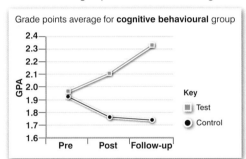

Grade points average for **cognitive behavioural** group

Key
- ■ Test
- ● Control

The findings found a significant impact on both academic performance and how the trainee accountants saw themselves, in comparison with the control group. Furthermore, in the follow up study the findings continued to produce excellent results with a wide gap between the cognitive behavioural group and the control group. The study also showed that the cognitive behavioural coaching intervention enhanced overall well-being as well as performance.

The results demonstrate the need for all four structures of the house of change to be in place to bring about lasting change.

EVALUATION OF EFFECTIVENESS

MATTEO'S RESULT

We finish with the concluding case study of Matteo's journey.

Six months after the initial evaluation, the coach asked Matteo to complete the EQ-i emotional intelligence assessment again to see if there had been any significant changes. In addition, his manager, team members, peers and anyone who worked with him were asked to complete an EI multi-rater feedback assessment (BarOn EQ360) to see if there was any congruency between Matteo and his raters.

Findings: Matteo's EI scores were noticeably congruent with his raters' scoring in the areas of interpersonal skills and impulse control. His coaching had used a combination of cognitive behavioural techniques and he had been encouraged to consciously practise self-reflection by keeping a thoughts journal. These measures had helped him learn to stop and notice how his thoughts were making him feel and react.

In a nutshell – feedback from the 360 demonstrated Matteo had made a positive change in the way he related to his team.

FINAL THOUGHTS & REFLECTIONS

I hope you have enjoyed reading this pocketbook, and I encourage you to give CB coaching a try with your clients, or even coaching yourself.

Drawing on my own research, training and work as a coach has led me to explore more robust, psychologically researched and evidence-based forms of coaching. Coaching that will provide a coach or client with the tools and techniques with which to build authentic, emotionally intelligent behaviours that are sustainable and not short-lived or acted out.

CB coaching moves the coaching industry towards a more mature approach where emotions, feelings, thoughts and beliefs, if tackled, offer an individual a solid foundation for real behaviour change to take place. In addition, by allowing them to become their own coach, it will lead to greater equilibrium both in their personal and professional lives.

REFERENCES & FURTHER READING

The Feeling Good Handbook, David Burns, Plume, 1999
Emotional Intelligence – Why it can matter more than IQ, Daniel Goleman, Bantam, 1995
Emotional Intelligence Pocketbook, Margaret Chapman, Management Pocketbooks, 2001
Psychometric Testing Pocketbook, Barry Cripps and Dorothy Spry, Management Pocketbooks, 2007
Life Coaching: A Cognitive-Behavioural Approach, Michael Neenan and Windy Dryden, Routledge, 2002
Motivational Interviewing, Preparing People for Change, William Miller and Stephen Rollnick,
Guilford Press, 2002
The Thinkers Guide To: The Art of Socratic Questioning, Richard Paul and Linda Elder,
Foundation for Critical Thinking, 2007
**Changing for Good: A Revolutionary Six Stage Program for Overcoming Bad Habits and Moving
Your Life Positively Forward**, J. Prochaska, J. Norcross and C DiClemente, Harper Paperbacks, 1995
Coach Yourself: It's Your Life What Are You Going To Do With It, Anthony Grant and Jane Greene,
Momentum, 2004

References

The Coaching Psychologist, Vol 3, No 2 August 2007. **Fiona Beddoes-Jones and Julia Miller**
*Coaching for Enhanced Performance: Comparing cognitive and behavioural approaches to coaching:
3rd International Spearman Seminar, Extending Intelligence: Enhancement and New Constructs, Sydney
2001.* **Anthony Grant**
*Our future in focus: A case study of developing team emotional intelligence in the public sector,
Competency and Emotional Intelligence, Vol 11, no 3, pp 37-42.* **Margaret Chapman**
Taking the temperature of coaching. **CIPD Survey (Summer 2009)**